THE
PHILOSOPHER'S
STONE

HYDROLITHVS SOPHICVS
SEV
AQVARIVM
SAPIENTVM,
Hoc est:
OPVSCVLVM CHYMI-
CVM, IN QVO VIA MON-
stratur, Materia nominatur, & Pro-
cessus describitur, quomodo videlicet
ad vniuersalem Tincturam per-
ueniendum, hactenus nun-
dum visum.
Publici emolumenti & vtilitatis
vniuersalis caussa typis publicis
subiectum.
ANNO M.DC.XXV.

HERMES.

R.LVLLI?

GEBER.

ROC:BACH.

MORIEN?

PARACELS?

Exact reproduction of the frontispiece
of an old book on alchemy.

THE
PHILOSOPHER'S STONE
Irrefutable Proofs of its Existence

by

PAPUS

Translated from the French by
Tau Phosphoros

TriadPress
Fox Lake, IL

The Philosopher's Stone: Irrefutable Proofs of its Existence

by Papus

Translated by Tau Phosphoros

Published September 2025.

ISBN: 978-1-946814-18-0

Triad Press, LLC
123 S. US Hwy. 12 #33
Fox Lake, IL 60020

Table of Contents

Foreword

A certain audacity is necessary to treat such a subject at the end of the 19th century.

We are, however, convinced in advance that the reader will forgive us in regard to our sincerity.

Indeed, we come to offer to the public not the conclusions of a mystical enthusiasm of a biased mind, but rather the result of a positive work worthy of being taken into consideration by all serious people.

First of all we are going to see what is meant by the word Philosopher's Stone, and for this we will have to summarize the opinion of the most educated alchemists. When you know the scientific significance of this expression, it will be necessary for us to see whether it is, or is not, in contradiction to the established facts of contemporary chemistry. Enlightened on these two points, we approach the History, seeking with the greatest impartiality whether the Philosopher's Stone has given any serious and irrefutable proofs of its existence, capable of being easily verified by the reader. This will be the capital point of our work, the raison d'être of our whole study.

It is then that we can say some words on the great alchemical family, on the doctrines of its members, and on the remnants of their science existing still in the architecture of our old monuments and the rites of certain high grades of Freemasonry. Finally, a small list of the most useful books for the beginner will end our research.

Such is the plan of our work. We hope that it will not make the reader regret too much the few minutes that his reading will take him, and we pray to excuse in advance the imperfections which may be found herein, solely imputable to the author of the study, and not to the doctrines or to the masters studied.

Part I

What is meant by Philosopher's Stone?

This question, so simple at first sight, is nevertheless rather difficult to resolve. Let us open the serious dictionaries, let us traverse the grave compilations of the rare scholars who have deigned to treat this subject. The conclusion is easy enough to pose: Philosopher's Stone, transmutation of the metals, equals *Ignorance, Imposture, Madness.*

If, however, we reflect that on the whole, in order to speak of *cloths*, it is better to go to a clothier than to a doctor of literature, the idea will perhaps come to us to see what the alchemists think on the question.

Now, in the midst of deliberate obscurities and numerous symbols which fill their treatises, a point upon which they are all in agreement is the definition and the qualities of the Philosopher's Stone.

The perfect Philosopher's Stone is a red powder which bas the property to transform all the impurities of nature.

It is generally believed that it can only be used, according to the alchemists, to change lead or mercury into gold. This is an error. The alchemical theory derives from sources much too speculative to localize its effect thus. Evolution being one of the great laws of nature, as Hermeticism taught several centuries ago, the Philosopher's Stone makes to evolve rapidly what the natural forms take long years to produce; that is why it acts, say the adepts, upon the vegetable and animal kingdoms as well as upon the mineral kingdom, and may be called *medicine of the three kingdoms.*

Physically it would be a red powder, similar in consistency to the chloride of gold, and with the odor of calcinated sea salt. Presently, moreover, we will have the occasion to return to this subject. As it is in the transformation of the *base*, lead and mercury, into gold that this Stone is to be most often used, let us look into what this operation consists.

Chemically, it is a simple increase of density if the unity of matter is admitted, an idea quite popular among the contemporary philosophical chemists. Indeed, the problem to resolve consists in transforming a body with the density of 13.6, like mercury, into a body with the density of 19.5, like gold. Is this hypothesis of *transmutation* at variance with the most recent notions of chemistry?

This is what we are going to see.

Part II

Does current chemistry allow itself to deny the existence of the Philosopher's Stone?

Two contemporary chemists have pushed their investigations into the obscure domain of alchemy; they are Messrs. Figuier, in 1853, who published *l'Alchimie et les Alchimistes*, a book on which we will presently have the occasion to speak, and the professor M. Berthelot, member of the Institute, who made appear, in 1885, the *Origines de l'Alchimie*.

These two learned officials, the latter especially, have authority in the matter and their opinion deserves to be heard by all serious persons.

Both consider alchemy and its aim as beautiful dreams, worthy of times past.

Both formally deny the existence of the philosopher's stone (although Figuier unknowingly proves its existence). And yet they declare that scientifically the thing cannot be denied *a priori*. Thus Figuier says:

"In our present state of understanding, one cannot prove in an absolutely rigorous manner that the transmutation of metals is impossible. Some circumstances are opposed to rejecting the alchemical opinion as an absurdity in contradiction to the facts."

(*l'Alchimie et les Alchimistes*, p. 353.)

M. Berthelot, in several passages of his book, shows that far from being opposed to contemporary chemistry, the alchemical theory tends, on the contrary, to replace today the primitive notions of chemical philosophy. Here are some extracts to support it:

"Through the mystical explanations and the symbols with which the alchemists envelop themselves, we can catch a glimpse of the essential theories of their philosophy; which are reduced in sum to a small number of clear, plausible ideas, and of which certain ones offer a strange analogy to the concepts of our time."

(Berthelot, *les Origines de 1'Alchimie*, p.280.)

"Why couldn't we form sulphur with oxygen, form selenium and tellurium with sulphur, through processes of proper condensation? Why couldn't tellurium and selenium be changed inversely into sulphur, and this latter metamorphosized into oxygen? Nothing, indeed, is opposed to this *a priori*."

(*Ibid.*, p. 297.)

"Assuredly, I repeat, nothing can assert that the fabrication of well known simple bodies is impossible *a priori*."

(*Ibid.*, p. 321.)

All this shows well enough that the Philosopher's Stone is not fatally impossible, even in the opinion of the contemporary scholars. Now we must seek whether we have any positive proofs of its existence.

Part III

*Proofs of the existence of the Philosopher's Stone.
Discussion of their validity.*

We assert that the Philosopher's Stone has given irrefutable proofs of its existence, and we are going to set out the facts upon which our convictions are based.

We have stated the facts; for one cannot consider as absolutely serious the demonstrations drawn from more or less solid reasoning. It is in the domain of history that the assertions are always easy to verify in every era, and because of this, even truly irrefutable. We are going, then, to set forth the arguments invoked by the adversaries of alchemy against transmutation, and the facts alone will be able to victoriously refute each of these objections.

It is Geoffroy the elder who was charged in 1722 to perform the process of the alchemists before the Academy. If his memoirs are to be believed, the numerous histories of transmutation upon which the adepts base their faith are easily explained by trickery. Uncontested philosophers such as Paracelsus or Raymond Lulle left their abstract speculations for a moment in order to make some clever turns of slight of hand before some good, astonished simpletons. However, let us analyze the means of deception that they laid out, and seek to determine experimental conditions bringing these arguments to naught.

The alchemists, in order to deceive the assistants, use:

1. *Crucibles with a double base;*
2. *Hollow charcoal or rods filled with gold powder;*
3. *Chemical reactions unknown then, but perfectly known today.*

For any one of these conditions to be realized, it must necessarily be that the alchemist is present at the operation or has touched beforehand the instruments employed.

Therefore, in the experimental determination of a transmutation, the absence of the alchemist will be the first and most indispensable of the conditions.

It is necessary, moreover, that he has not had in hand any of the objects which will be used in this transmutation.

Finally, in order to respond to the final argument, it is indispensable that the notions of contemporary chemistry be unable to explain normally the result obtained.

So that our work finds an even more solid base of evidence, it is necessary to put the reader in a position to easily verify all our assertions. That is why we will draw our arguments from one sole work, easy to find: *Alchimie et les Alchimistes*, by Louis Figuier.

Let us recall, before going further, the most essential conditions.

1. *Absence of the Alchemist;*
2. *That he has not touched anything that the operator used;*

3. *That the deed be unexplainable by contemporary chemistry.*

And we may add also:

4. *That the operator cannot be suspected of complicity.*

∴

Let us open the book of Mr. Figuier, edition of 1854, chapter III, page 206.

Here we find, not one, but three facts answering all our conditions, and that we are going to discuss one by one.

Not only is the operator not an alchemist, but is considered a scholar, a declared enemy of alchemy, which answers even more strongly our fourth condition, Let us speak first of Helvetius and his transmutation; we cite textually Figuier:

"Jean-Fréderic Schweitzer, known under the Latin name Helvetius, was one of the most decided adversaries of alchemy; he had even become celebrated by a writing against the sympathetic powder of the chevalier Digby. On December 27, 1666, he received at the Hague a visit from a stranger, dressed, he said, as a commoner from the north of Holland, and who obstinately refused to make known his name. This stranger announced to Helvetius that upon the report of his dispute with the chevalier Digby, he had hastened to bring him the material proofs of the existence of the Philosopher's Stone. In a long conversation, the adept defended the Hermetic principles, and in order to lift the doubts from his adversary, he showed him in a little ivory box, the Philosopher's Stone. It was a powder of a metallic color of sulphur. In vain did Helvetius implore the unknown to demonstrate to him by the fire the virtues of his powder. The alchemist resisted at every instance and withdrew while promising to return in three weeks.

"All while talking with this man and while examining the Philosopher's Stone, Helvetius had had the cleverness to detach some particles thereof and held them under his fingernail. Scarcely was he alone that he was eager to assay the virtues thereof. He put some melted lead into a crucible and made the projection. But all was dissipated in smoke; nothing remained in the crucible but a little lead and vitrified earth.

"Judging then this man as an impostor, Helvetius had nearly forgotten the adventure when, three weeks later and on the marked day, the stranger reappeared. He refused again to do the operation himself, but yielding to the prayers of the physician, he made him a gift of a little bit of his stone, barely the size of a grain of millet. And as Helvetius expressed the fear that so little a quantity of substance could not have the least property, the alchemist, finding the gift still too magnificent, took back half saying that the remainder was sufficient to transmute an ounce and a half of lead. At the same time he took care to make known in detail the precautions necessary for the success of the work, and recommended especially at the moment of the projection to surround the Philosopher's Stone with a little wax in order to shield it from the smoke of the lead. Helvetius understood in this moment why the transmutation that he had attempted had failed in his hands; he had not wrapped the stone in wax and consequently neglected an indispensable precaution.

"The stranger promised furthermore to return the next day in order to assist in the experiment.

"The next day Helvetius waited uselessly; the entire day passed without seeing anyone. When the evening came, the physician's wife no longer being able to contain her impatience, convinced her husband to attempt the operation alone. The attempt was carried out by Helvetius in the presence of his wife and son.

"He melted down an ounce and a half of lead, projected upon the melted metal the Stone wrapped in wax, covered the crucible with its lid, and left it exposed for a quarter of an hour to the action of the fire. At the end of this time, the metal had acquired the beautiful green color of melted gold; cast and re-cooled, it became a magnificent yellow.

"All the goldsmiths of the Hague estimated very highly the degree of this gold. Povelius, assayer general of the monies of Holland, treated it seven times with antimony without it diminishing in weight."

Such is the narration that Helvetius had made himself on this adventure. The terms and the minute details of his account exclude on his part any suspicion

on imposture. He was so astonished with this success that it is on this occasion that he wrote *Vitulus aureus* in which he related this event and defends alchemy.

⁚

This fact answers to all the required conditions. However, Mr. Figuier, sensing how difficult it was to explain, added some explanations in a later edition (1860).

Wishing to find everywhere the fraud *a priori*, here is his principal argument:

The alchemist has a paid accomplice who comes to put into one of the crucibles of Helvetius a compound of gold easily decomposed by the heat. Is it necessary to show the artlessness of this objection?

1. How does one choose just the crucible that Helvetius will take?
2. How are we to believe that this latter is stupid enough not to recognize an empty crucible from a full one, or an alloy from a metal?
3. Why not take the care to re-read the account of the facts? Mr. Figuier would have seen two important points:

First the following phrase: *he took an ounce and a half of lead.* This indicates that he has weighed it, that he has handled it, which would have put him in a position to easily verify whether it was truly from the lead.

4. Then this little detail: *he covered the crucible with its lid*, which prevents any subsequent evaporation.
5. Even supposing that Helvetius had truly been deceived; that he, experienced scholar, had

taken lead for gold, the proof of the transmutation stands out no less evident, for the critics always forget the following fact:

If there exists an alloy hiding the gold within it, the ingot, after evaporation or oxidation of the impure metal, will weigh much less than the metal initially employed.

If, on the contrary, there is adjunction of gold by some process, the ingot will weigh *much more* than the metal initially employed.

Now, the transmutation of Bérigard of Pisa, which will be found hereafter, proves irrefutably the inanity of these arguments.

Finally, in order to destroy forever the assertions of Mr. Figuier, it suffices to note that the goldsmiths of the Hague as well as the assayer of the monies of Holland confirmed the absolute purity of the gold, which would be impossible if there had been any alloy. Thus falls from itself the explanation that the critic gives of this fact.

"We cannot hardly explain today these events but by admitting that the mercury which was used or the crucible that was employed contained a certain quantity of gold concealed with a marvelous ability."

(Louis Figuier, *Ibid.*, p. 210)

We have said that *one sole fact*, well proven, would suffice to demonstrate the existence of the Philosopher's Stone, and there exist three in the same conditions. Let us look at the other two:

Here is the account of Bérigard of Pisa, cited likewise by Figuier, p. 211:

"I will relate," Bérigard of Pisa tells us, "what has happened to me formerly, when I strongly doubted that it was possible to convert mercury into gold. An able man, wishing to lift my doubt in this regard, gave me a mass of powder whose color was rather similar to that of wild poppy, and whose odor recalled that of calcinated sea salt. In order to destroy every suspicion of fraud, I bought the crucible, the charcoal, and the mercury myself from various merchants so as not to have to fear that there was gold in any of these materials, which the alchemical charlatans often do. On ten large parts of mercury, I added a little powder. I exposed all this to a rather strong fire, and in a little while the mass was found entirely converted into nearly the same weight of gold, which was recognized as very pure by the assays of various goldsmiths. If this event had not occurred to me without witnesses, outside the presence of foreign arbitrators, I would have been able to suspect fraud. But I can assure with confidence that the thing has occurred as I relate it."

Here again it is a scholar who operates; but he knows the ruses of the charlatans and employs all the precautions imaginable to avoid them. Finally, let us also cite the transmutation of Van Helmont in order to edify in all respects the impartial reader:

In 1618, in his laboratory of Vilvoorde, near Brussels, Van Helmont received from an unknown hand a quarter grain of Philosopher's Stone. It came from an adept who, succeeding in the discovery of the secret, desired to convince the illustrious scholar whose works honored his era of its reality.

Van Helmont carried out the experiment himself alone in his laboratory. With the quarter grain of powder that he had received from the unknown he transformed into gold eight ounces of mercury. It must be admitted that such a feat was an argument nearly without replica to invoke in favor of the existence of the Philosopher's Stone. Van Helmont, the most able chemist of his time, was difficult to deceive. He was himself incapable of imposture, and he had not any interest in lying since he never drew the least profit from this observation.

Finally, the experiment having taken place outside of the presence of the alchemist, it is difficult to understand how the fraud had been able to slip past.

Van Helmont was so enlightened by this subject that he became an avowed partisan of alchemy. He gave in honor of this adventure the name of Mercurius to his newborn son. This Mercurius Van Helmont did not deny his alchemical baptism. He converted

Leibnitz to this opinion; for his whole life he sought the Philosopher's Stone and died without having found it, it is true, but a fervent apostle of it.

Let us return now to these three accounts, and we will verify that they answer the scientific questions posed. In fact:

Did the mercury or the lead contain the gold? I do not think so, seeing as:

1. Helvetius, who did not believe in alchemy any more than Van Helmont or Bérigard of Pisa,

who were in the same position, was not going to trifle with putting it there;

2. In no case had the alchemist touched the objects employed;

3. Finally, in the transmutation of Bérigard of Pisa, if the mercury had contained the gold and if the latter had remained alone after the volatilization of the first, the ingot obtained would have weighed much less than the mercury used, which it did not.

After these arguments, one could believe that the list is closed; not in the least. There remains yet one, dishonest, it is true, but all the more dangerous: *All these accounts, drawn from published books, are not the work of the signatory authors, but rather of capable impostor alchemists.*

That is certainly a terrible objection which seems to destroy all our work; but the truth may yet appear victoriously.

Indeed, there exists a letter from a third person as eminent as the others, the philosopher Spinoza, addressed to Jarrig Jellis. This letter proves irrefutably the reality of the experiment of Helvetius. Here is the important passage:

"Having spoken to Voss on the affair of Helvetius, he made fun of me, being astonished at seeing me occupied with such trifles. In order to have a clear mind on this, I went to the coiner Brechtel, who had assayed the gold. This one assured me that, during its melting, the gold had even increased in weight when silver was thrown in. It must be, therefore, that this gold, which has changed the silver into new gold, was of a most peculiar nature. Not only Brechtel, but also other persons who had assisted with the assay, assured me that the thing had happened in this way. I then returned to Helvetius himself who showed me the gold and the crucible still containing a little gold attached to the inside. He told me that he had barely thrown upon the melted lead a quarter grain of wheat of Philosopher's Stone. He added that he would make known this history to everyone. It appears that this adept had already done the same experiment at Amsterdam where he could still be found. That is all the information that I have been able to get on this subject.

"Boorbourg, March 27, 1667.

"Spinoza."

(*Opera posthuma*, p. 553)

Such are the facts that have led us to this conviction: The Philosopher's Stone has given irrefutable proofs of its existence, unless one denies forever the witnesses of the texts, history, and men.

Part IV
The Alchemist

We have spoken much of the Philosopher's Stone; let us now say some words on its fortunate possessor: the Alchemist.

One generally imagines this man living in a perpetual search for the impossible in the midst of burning furnaces, stuffed crocodiles, sinister owls, and bewitched cats. It suffices, however, to open their books, to see the manner by which they themselves represent their furnaces and their laboratories in order to verify that this is a profound error attributable to the prejudices of the masses.[1]

The true alchemist is a philosopher educated enough to cross, without being affected, the most troubled and difficult epochs.[2] He is the sacred depository of all this marvelous science taught of old in the venerated sanctuaries of India and Egypt.[3] He must know enough to veil it in order to escape the jealous glance of the clerical despot who smells in him the enemy and who watches him closely.

It is when the Inquisition persecutes unmercifully every trace of knowledge, that the Hermetic philosopher veils his writings even more under symbols and mysterious figures; not enough, however, so that the conscientious seeker cannot easily understand. This is the origin of the deliberate obscurities that one

---

[1] See the plate at the head of our study.

[2] Louis Lucas, *le Roman Alchimique*.

[3] Papus, *Traité élémentaire de Science occulte*.

encounters in the works of the adepts.

What use do they make of the immense wealth that the knowledge of this marvelous secret may procure for them?

One of the elementary rules of the science called occult, teaches that, in order to be master of something, one must be able to consider it with the greatest indifference.

The one who desires the Philosopher's Stone for the riches that it procures and for his material good, has considerable chances to never possess it.

Thus, the esoteric tradition represents the alchemist to us simple dressed and always traveling, giving alms to the beggars and to the kings, and by this showing himself superior to these latter.[4]

If we believe the accounts of the contemporaries, the alchemist Nicolas Flamel, possessor of immense wealth, used it only on pious or charitable foundations and ate, as well as his wife, boiled vegetables, in the coarsest earthenware dish.

We will find these ideas put into practice until the middle of the 19th century when the alchemist Cyliani (1832) having, he relates, discovered the philosopher's stone at the end of forty years of work, living by a small private income very modestly after having had the temptation to offer the precious secret to the king Louis XVIII; his wife dissuaded him from it.[5]

Moreover, it suffices to examine the work of

---

[4] Eliphas Lévi, *Histoire de la Magie*.
[5] Cyliani, *Hermès dévoilé, 1832*.

Figuier to have numerous details on this subject.

The doctrine taught by the alchemists is in great part philosophical. The experiment ought only to serve as verification of the speculative theories announced in the most venerated books. That is why the adepts call the collection of their knowledge: Hermetic Philosophy.

The Hermetic Philosophy professes the unity of substance at the basis of all its demonstrations. There exists a *universal principle* spread throughout all the bodies whatever be their composition otherwise. It is the knowledge of this *universal principle* and putting it into practice which constitutes the secret of the great work and which renders different *ab initio* the alchemical experiments from the works of the ordinary chemists, that the Hermetic philosophers consider as laboratory shop-boys.

The occult force has received a multitude of names in the alchemical works: it is the *Telesme* of Hermes[6], the *Aur* of the Kabbalists[7], the *Ruach Elohim* of Moses[8], the *Universal Mercury* of the alchemists[9], the *Astral Light* of the Occult Science[10], the *Movement* of Louis Lucas[11], etc., etc.

Moreover, this theory, to which the contemporary philosophers are led, comes to be restored to the light

---

[6] *The Emerald Tablet.*

[7] See Eliphas Lévi, *la Clef des grand mystères.*

[8] Fabre d'Olivet, *la Langue hébraïque restituée.*

[9] Crosset de la Haumeris, *les Secrets les plus* cachés (6th treatise).

[10] E. Lévi, *Dogme et Rituel de Haute Magie.*

[11] Louis Lucas, *Chimie Nouvelle.*

of day in all its beauty through the works of the Theosophical Society under the inspiration of the Hindu adepts.[12]

One will also find details on this interesting subject in a very beautiful study by Mr. de Rochas entitled *les Doctrines chimiques au XVIIe siècle* and appearing in *Cosmos* in 1888.

Does there exist in our era some trace of this Hermetic philosophy and its teachings? Let us seek it.

---

[12] See H.P. Blavatsky, *Isis Unveiled* and *The Secret Doctrine*.

Part V
Vestige of Alchemy in Our Era

The alchemists worked in general alone until the 16th century. From this era, the initiation was given by more or less powerful secret societies. It is they who have left traces durable enough so that we can find them in our era.

Without wishing to speak of the Templars, prematurely destroyed, the most important and the best known of the Hermetic societies is without doubt the mysterious Fraternity of the Rose-Croix. It is under their impetus that English Freemasonry was founded, from where are derived all the modern initiations.[13]

Freemasonry presents us even today the living traditions of Hermeticism in several of its high grades, and it is from this point of view that the B∴ Ragon has particularly studied it in his *Maçonnerie occulte*.

Thus the lost and rediscovered word of the 18th degree of Scottish Masonry, INRI, is explained eso-terically by an alchemical aphorism:

Igne Natura Renovatur Integra[14]

Nature is renewed in its integrity by fire.

This *fire* is not the common fire; it is the *universal force* of which we have spoken, represented also by the G at the center of the Blazing Star.[15]

---

[13] Ragon, *Orthodoxie Maçonnique.*

[14] See Papus, *Franc-Maçons et Théosophes.*

[15] See Ragon, *la Messe et ses Mystères.*

The 22nd degree (Royal Axe) and the 28° (Prince Adept) are also filled with actual traditions of the Hermetic science.[16]

Beyond these traditions, preserved without the knowledge of those who possess them, several monuments of Paris are also positive proofs of the teachings of the Hermetic philosophy.

Let us cite in the first rank of this point of view the *Saint-Jacque Tower*, then the Stained-Glass Windows of Sainte-Chapelle; finally the *Gate of Notre Dame de Paris*.[17]

Finally, the 19th century has seen several convinced alchemists born. Let us cite first Cyliani, author of *Hermès Dévoilé* (1832), in which he asserts to have discovered the Philosopher's Stone, and gives in alchemical style the means to fabricate it. It is curious to see this symbolic style employed even in our day.

After him, we must cite Théodore Tiffereau, old preparer of chemistry at the School of Nantes, author of a memoire addressed to the Academy, entitled: *Les Metaux ne sont pas des corps simples* (1853), in 8-vo).

Then comes the least serious of all, Cambriel, author of an evil treatise bearing the title of *l'Alchimie en 19 leçons*.

Such are the representatives of alchemy in our era. Do there exist any others in the Occident, do they exist

---

[16] Albert Pike, *Marals and Dogma of Freemasonry*, Charleston, 1881, p. 340 and following.

[17] See the drawing and explanation of the alchemical Hieroglyph of the front gate of Notre Dame in the *Traité élémentaire de Science Occulte* by Papus, plate VI.

in the societies of Hermeticism? This we cannot say.

Our monograph will not be complete if we end without at least indicating all the books most useful to those who wish to push further these curious studies.

This is what we are going to attempt to do.

Part VI
How One Can Study Alchemy

The first book that we recommend reading in its entirety is the one by Louis Figuier entitled *l'Alchimie et les Alchimistes*. Although the author poses as a decided adversary of the Hermetic Philosophy, his book is very well done on the whole and, except for some errors of details, merits the trouble to be taken into serious consideration. The historical partis especially remarkable and its reading leads inevitably to demonstrating with evidence the existence of the Philosopher's Stone. It is therefore over all for the historical part that the work of Louis Figuier ought to be studied.

For the theoretical part and alchemical symbolism, one will find some rather long details in the *Traité élémentaire de Science occulte*[18] (pp. 90 to 106) in the article "Alchimie."

It is then that one will be able to read the work of a true alchemist and take cognizance of this bizarre and figurative style. We strongly recommend to take up for this point of view the work of Cyliani cited in the previous chapter.

One will see that even in the 19th century the symbolic language is still in use despite contemporary chemistry; one will also be able to get a clear idea, through the account of the forty years of suffering and research of the alchemist, of the difficulty of the work

---

[18] 3rd ed., Carré, 58, rue St-André-des-Arts.

undertaken.

One will find this volume, become very rare, at the Bibliothèque Nationale (letter R).

Finally, the elementary instruction will be quite complete if one wants to read *l'Histoire de la Philosophie hermétique* by Langlet du Fresnoy and the authors reproduced in the two volumes of the *Bibliothèque des Philosophes chimiques* by Salmon (1753).

As there exist more than three thousand volumes on Alchemy, we believe to have to limit ourselves to giving the most important ones. Those who wish to become practicing alchemists, whom I feel most sorry for, must take cognizance of the masters[19], especially the works of Geber, Raymond Lulle, Basil Valentine, Paracelsus, and Van Helmont.

---

[19] See the plate representing the principal ones among them with their esoteric attributes according to an old treatise on Alchemy.

Conclusion

Having reached the end of our work, we hope to have attained the aim pursued: *To demonstrate that the Philosopher's Stone is not only possible, but that it has existed and has given irrefutable proofs of its existence.*

We pray the serious people, who are not animated by any set purpose or preconceived idea, to consider well our assertions, to verify their authenticity in the original books, which is easy at the Bibliothèque Nationale, and to see whether these are *irrefutable proofs* or rather simple conjectures stripped of any stable foundation. The love of truth has led us to defend the alchemists, these modest philosophers too little known and too slandered. May we incite some seeker more educated than ourselves to develop and expand this most particular genre of studies.

Moreover, we are witness to a true renaissance of antiquity. The phenomena, so curious a suggestion, come to destroy well the anticipate conclusions, and perhaps the 20th century will finally see constituted the Synthesis through the alliance of the *positivist physics* of the Occident with the *idealist metaphysics* of the Orient. May the day be near when all the philosophies will re-enter into the *Unity* of one same Faith, when *Science* and *Faith* will, by their alliance, give birth to one sole synthesized TRUTH!

.

www.ingramcontent.com/pod-product-compliance
Lightning Source LLC
Chambersburg PA
CBHW021149020426
42331CB00005B/975